Racing Story

**Read the story, then flip the book over
to complete some awesome activities!**

First published by Parragon in 2012
Parragon
Queen Street House
4 Queen Street
Bath BA1 1HE, UK
www.parragon.com

Written by Susan Amerikaner
Illustrated by Scott Tilley, Andrew Phillipson, Janelle Bell-Martin,
Dan Gracey, Seung Beom Kim and the Disney Storybook Artists
Edited by Samantha Crockford
Designed by Karl Tall
Production by Sarah Brown

ISBN 978-1-4454-4801-5

Printed in China

Rematch!

PaRragon

Bath • New York • Singapore • Hong Kong • Cologne • Delhi
Melbourne • Amsterdam • Johannesburg • Auckland • Shenzhen

Lightning McQueen and Francesco Bernoulli had challenged each other to a race in Monza, Italy – Francesco's hometown.

"Benvenuto!" said Francesco. "Your plane was late, but this is no surprise. You will be late crossing the finish line, too."

Lightning smiled. Then he whispered to Mater,
"I am so beating him – right here on his own turf!"

As they left the airport, the cars were surrounded by photographers. "Everyone loves Francesco. He has too many fans," said Francesco.

"Nobody has more fans than Lightning!" Mater piped up.

Francesco rolled his eyes.

"We will prove it!" said Luigi. "Lightning gets hundreds of fan letters each day. Guido, bring the mailbags!"

Guido **zoomed** off!

Guido returned with mailbags overflowing with fan letters.

Lightning was a little embarrassed.
"Oh, it's really not that big of a deal," he said.

"You are right, Lightning," said Francesco.

"It is no big deal because Francesco has
much, much more fan mail!"

"Letters are great," said Lightning. "But we like to get some fender-to-fender time with our fans whenever we can."

Lightning and his friends greeted all the cars who were lined up to see them. Mater really got the fans going.

They began chanting: **"Light-NING! Light-NING!"**

"Questo e' ridicolo!" mumbled Francesco. "And what about autographs?" he asked. "Watch – and be amazed."

Francesco started spinning his wheels and spewing out
hundreds of autographed photos of himself to his fans.

"See? Francesco always gets things done at three hundred
kilometres an hour."

After the two racers finished greeting their fans, they drove to a café.

"Hey, Mr Francesco, nobody drinks oil faster than Lightning," said Mater.

"What?" said Lightning. "Mater, I can't drink..."

"C'mon buddy, show 'em what I done taught you!" said Mater.

Lightning sighed and managed to finish a can of oil in a few gulps.

Francesco was not impressed.
"Francesco never guzzles," he said.
"Oil should be savoured."

Lightning cruised over to Francesco. "How about a warm up before the big race – just you and me?" he asked.

Francesco nodded. "Ah, good idea, Lightning! Try to keep up, if you…"

Before Francesco could finish, Lightning was a red streak down the road!
"**Ka-*ciao***, Francesco!" yelled Lightning.

Francesco was just about to catch up with Lightning when he nearly spun out on a left turn.

"How do you make those left turns so well?" Francesco asked Lightning.

"Get equipped with some treaded tyres," said Lightning. "Then **turn right to go left.** A very good friend taught me that once."

They finally stopped to rest. Francesco sighed. "Ahh, Italia is beautiful, no? Just like Francesco!"

Lightning chuckled. "Do you always think about yourself?" he asked.

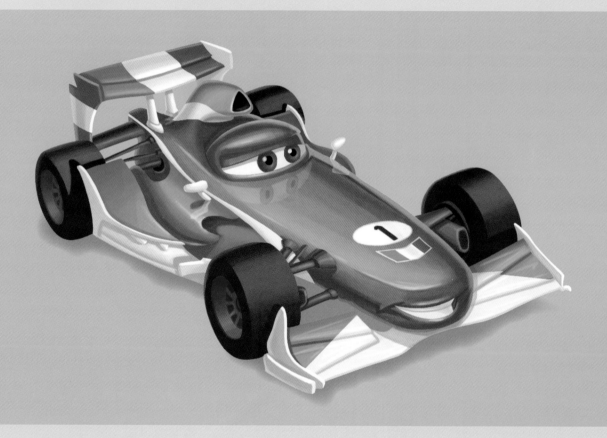

"Of course," said Francesco. "On the racetrack, Francesco only thinks about himself and doing his best. This is why he **always wins!"**

The next day was the big race. Finally, the world would find out who was the fastest race car! When the flag dropped, the fans went wild!

Francesco came out of the first left turn ahead of Lightning. He showed off his new treaded tyres. "Perhaps Lightning has taught Francesco too well!" Lightning couldn't help but smile.

The racers entered the Monza arena and made a pit stop. As Lightning zoomed out of the pits, he got distracted by the camera flashes and the screaming fans. Suddenly Lightning remembered what Francesco had said about focusing on himself and doing his best. Lightning looked straight ahead and took the lead!

As the two cars crossed the finish line, the crowd gasped.

"**Ka-chow**!" yelled Lightning. "I won!"

"You mean **ciao bella**," said Francesco. "Francesco won!"

According to the judges, the race was a... **TIE!!!**

The cars tried to figure out what to do.

Then Francesco shouted, "No more talk! Talk is slow.

What do we do? **We race!**"

"That's a great idea!" said Lightning. "We'll race in Radiator Springs!"

Then the two fastest cars in the world **zoomed** away together… to race again another day.

The End

Now close the book and flip it over to complete some **awesome activities!**

Action-Packed Activities

Complete the activities, then flip the book over to read an awesome story!

Bath · New York · Singapore · Hong Kong · Cologne · Delhi
Melbourne · Amsterdam · Johannesburg · Auckland · Shenzhen

Lightning McQueen

Lightning looks awesome in his racing colours. Use this picture as a guide to colour in Lightning on the opposite page.

KA-CHOWW!

Odd one out

Mater is Lightning's best friend. Can you tell which one of these Maters is the odd one out?

A

B

C

Answer on page 31

Shadow match

Can you match each member of Lightning's pit crew to their shadow?

1

A

2

B

3

C

Answers on page 31

5

Count the cars

Francesco is a super-fast racer. How many pictures of him can you count? Write your answer in the box below.

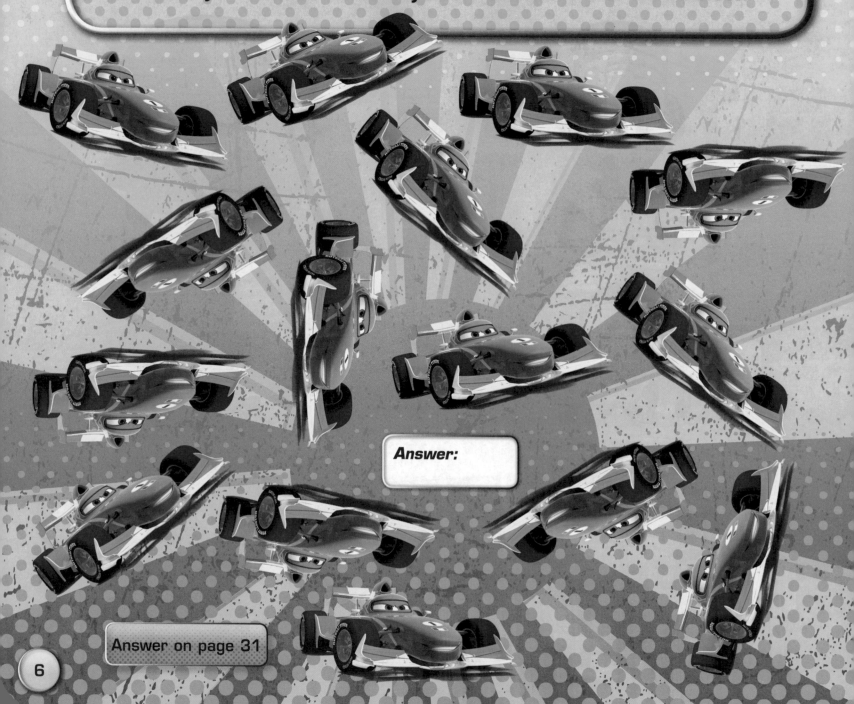

Answer:

Answer on page 31

Amazing maze

Finn McMissile is trying to meet up with his fellow agent, Holley Shiftwell. Can you find the correct route through the maze to reach Holley?

Answers on page 31

Who is it?

Connect the dots to reveal the identity of this Brazilian race car. Once you've identified her, colour in the picture!

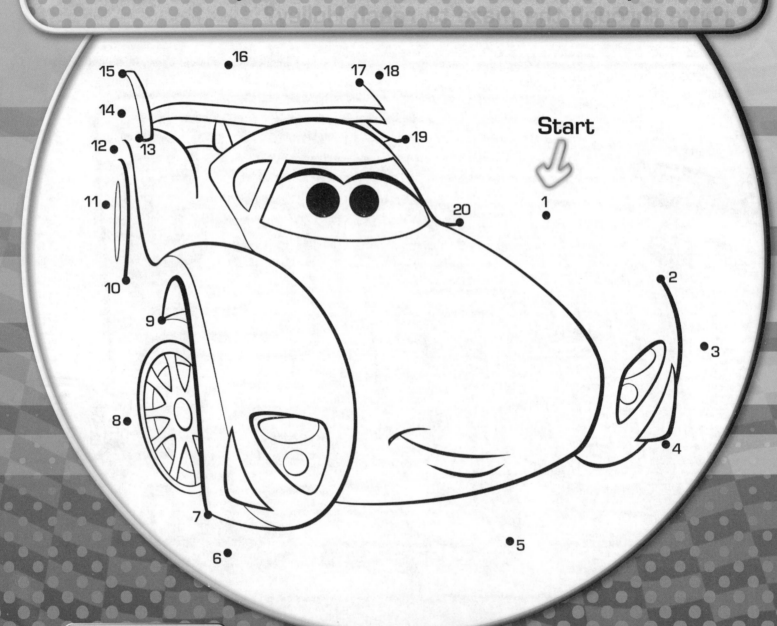

Start

Answer on page 31

Sushi pit-stop test!

Have a close look at this picture of a sushi bar in Tokyo. Count to ten, then turn the page and see if you can answer the question!

Sushi pit-stop test!

Did you look closely at the picture on the previous page? There are 6 things that have changed in the picture below. Can you see what they are? Circle the changes.

Answer on page 31

Word play

How many words can you make from the letters in this Italian racer's name?

Francesco

Green machine!

Fillmore lives next door to Sarge. He sells organic fuel and loves Jimi Hendrix. Use this picture as a guide and colour Fillmore on the opposite page.

All tangled up

Guido is looking for Luigi. Can you work out which of the lines he should follow?

A

B

C

Answer on page 31

Tokyo tyre shop

Lightning and Mater love being in Tokyo. Look closely at the picture, count to ten, then turn the page and see if you can answer the questions!

Memory test

What can you remember from the picture on the last page?

1 What colour is the car with the flat tyre?

2 How many teeth does Mater have?

3 How many blue petrol cans are there?

4 What number does Lightning have on his side?

5 What colour is the building behind the cars?

Answers on page 31

American road-star

Jeff Gorvette is one of America's greatest racers. Can you tell which two Jeffs are the same?

Answers on page 31

17

Shadow match

Can you match each of these bad cars to its shadow?

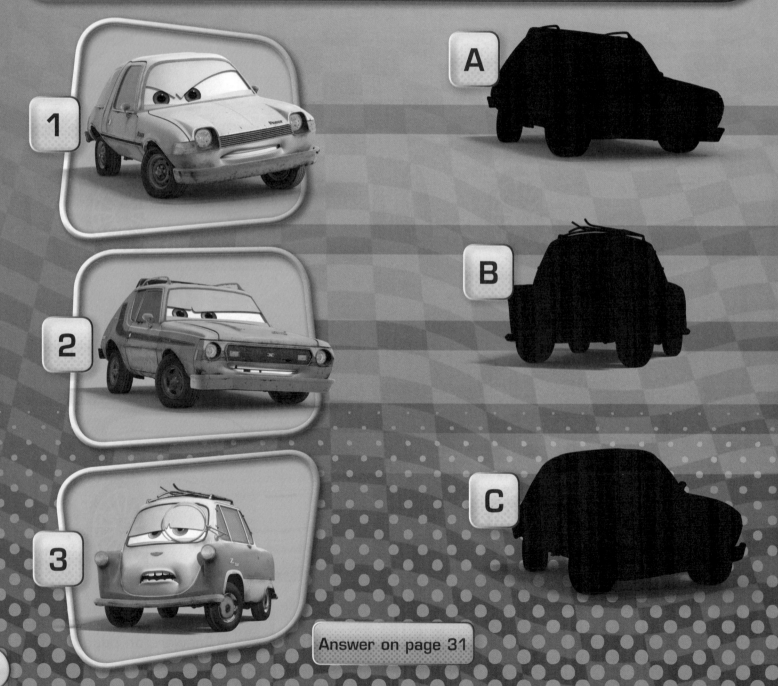

Answer on page 31

Amazing race

Mack must get Lightning to the big race on time.
Can you help him find a way through the maze?

Answers on page 31

Secret agent McMissile!

Agent Finn McMissile is on a secret mission.
Colour in this scene to help him out.

Flying to Italy

Lightning and Mater are on their way to Italy for the second race of the World Grand Prix. Colour them in.

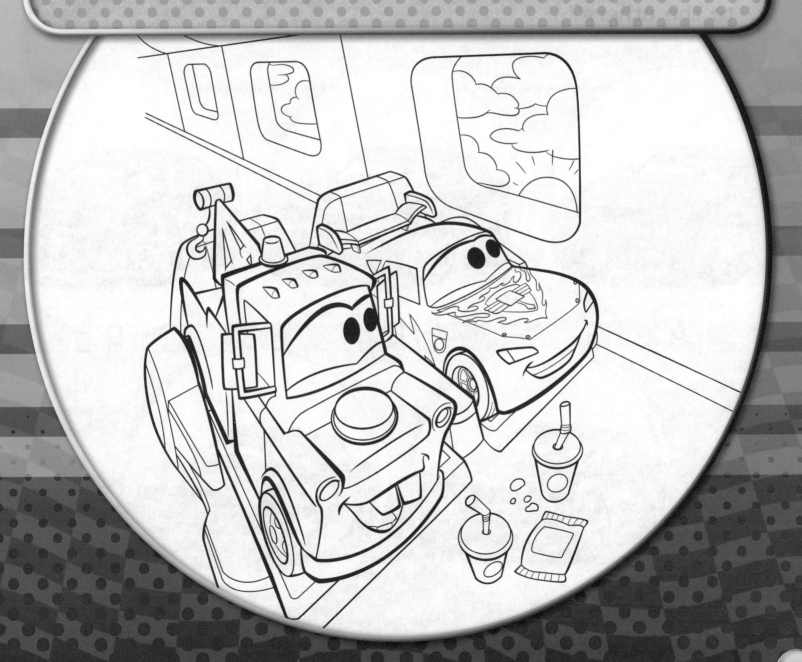

Fake Torque

Rod 'Torque' Redline is an American secret agent. But one of these is an imposter! Which picture is different to the others?

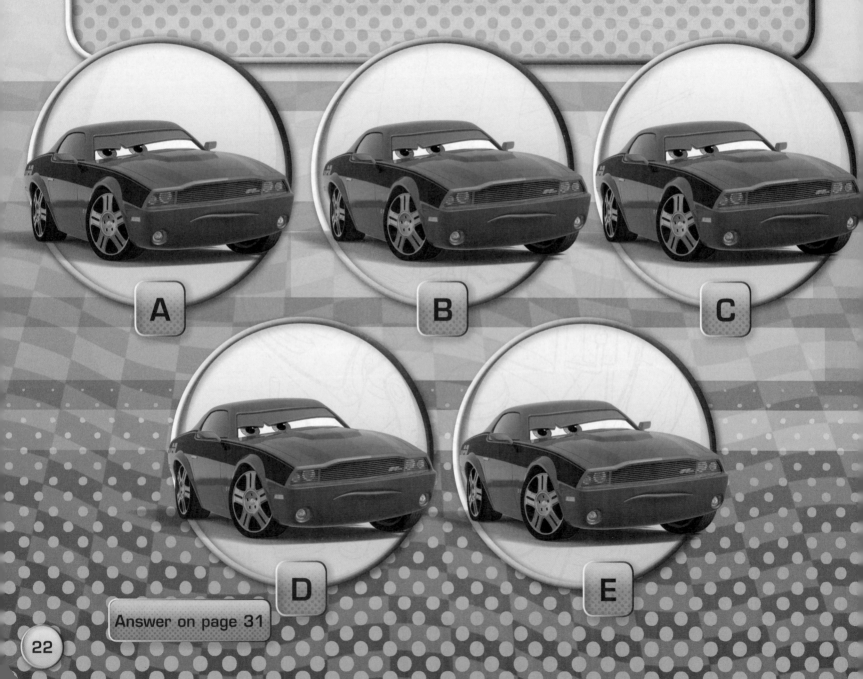

A

B

C

D

E

Answer on page 31

Guess who?

Take a look at this close-up of a World Grand Prix racer. Can you tell who it is? Complete his name in the box!

SH_ T_ _OR_K_

Answers on page 31

Count the caminos

Miguel Camino is a Spanish super car. How many pictures of him can you count? Write your answer in the box below.

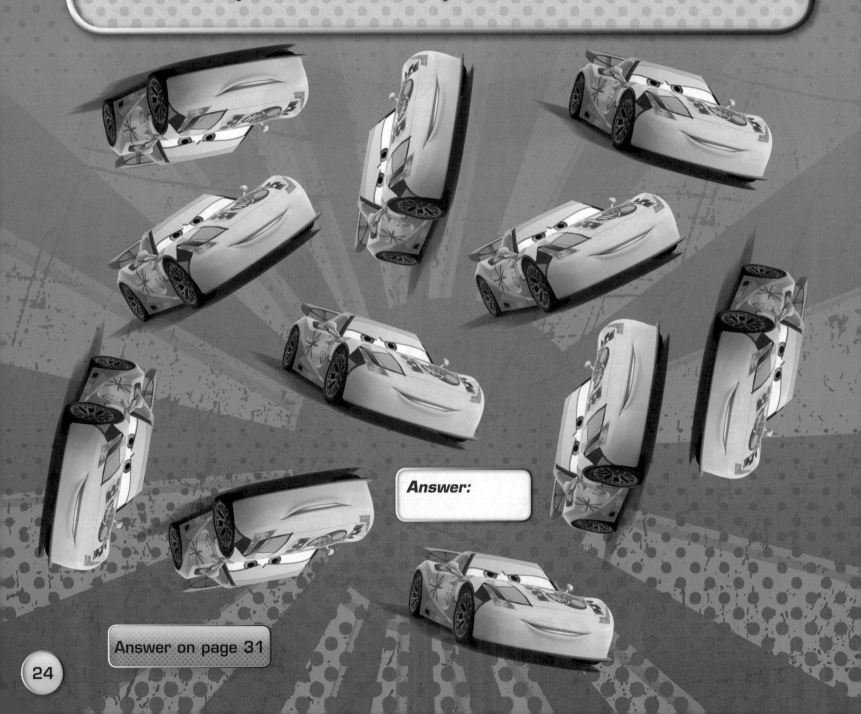

Answer:

Answer on page 31

Wordsearch whiz

Can you find all these Radiator Springs residents in the wordsearch below?

```
f o z y m e r g
f i l i i y z o
a z l z l r i g
g i z l y i t s
o i a y m m h a
l s r f g o f r
e m a t e r r g
s h e r i f f e
```

Mater

Fillmore

Sarge

Sally

Lizzie

Sheriff

Answers on page 31

Raoul's rally

Raoul ÇaRoule is the greatest rally car in the world and one of the favourites to win the World Grand Prix. Use this picture as a guide, and colour in Raoul on the opposite page.

Meeting the boss

Colour in this picture of Lightning meeting Sir Miles Axlerod at the World Grand Prix.

"I am speed!"

Get Lightning ready to race by colouring him in!

Unscramble challenge

Can you unscramble the names of these *Cars 2* characters?

A

ACRAL OLVEOS

B

IRS LEMSI DXEORLA

C

SOOSFPERR Z

D

EHOLYL FTELWLIHS

Answer on page 31

Answers

Page 4

B

Page 5

1 B
2 C
3 A

Page 6
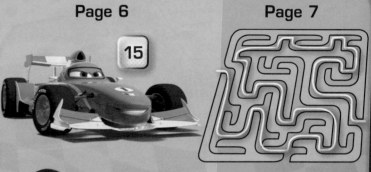
15

Page 7

Page 8
Carla Veloso

Page 10
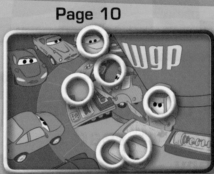

Page 14

B

Page 15
1 Yellow
2 Two
3 Five
4 95
5 Purple

Page 17

Page 18

1 C
2 A
3 B

Page 19

Page 22
D

Page 23
Shu Todoroki

Page 24
11

Page 25
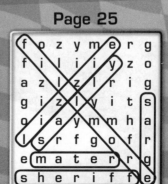
```
f o z y m e r g
f i l i i y z o
a z l z l r i g
g i z l y i t s
o i a y m m h a
l s r f g o f r
e m a t e r r g
s h e r i f f e
```

Page 30
A Carla Veloso
B Sir Miles Axlerod
C Professor Z
D Holley Shiftwell

31

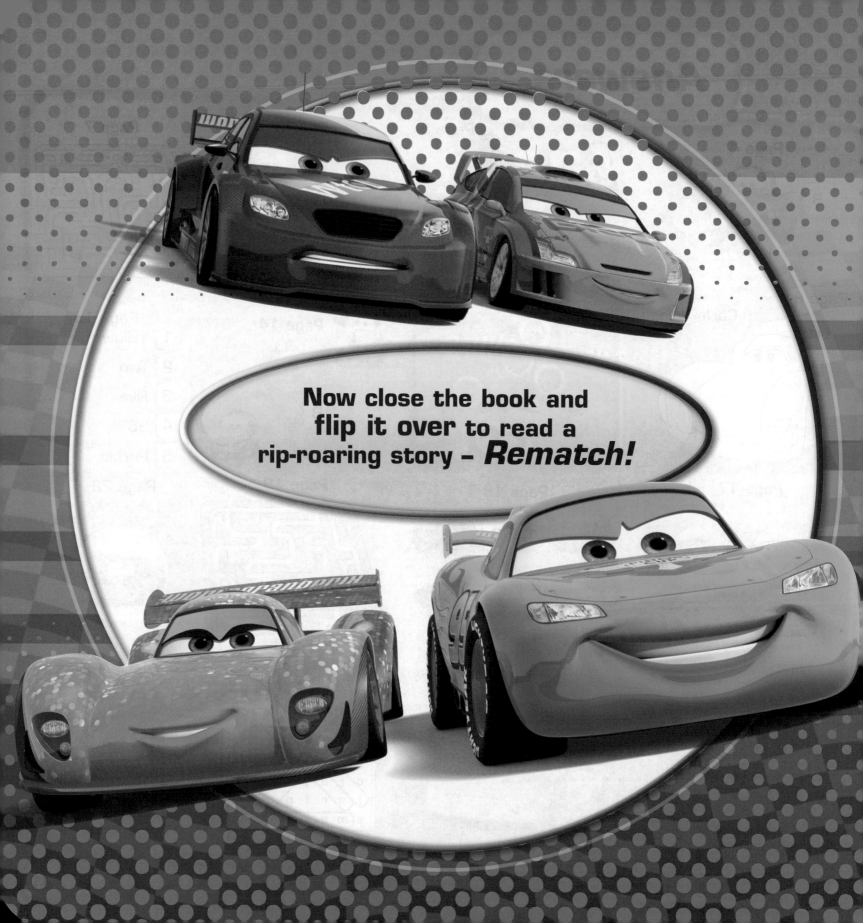

Now close the book and flip it over to read a rip-roaring story – *Rematch!*